Reflections

A Great Miracle Through The Storms

Patty P.

authorHOUSE®

AuthorHouse™
1663 Liberty Drive
Bloomington, IN 47403
www.authorhouse.com
Phone: 1 (800) 839-8640

Published by AuthorHouse 05/30/2020

ISBN: 978-1-4634-3649-0 (sc)
ISBN: 978-1-4634-3648-3 (hc)
ISBN: 978-1-4634-3647-6 (e)

Library of Congress Control Number: 2011912997

Print information available on the last page.

To those who encouraged me to keep the faith and to hold on to my dreams. Some of these people did not live to see my accomplishments, but there are some who did. Much gratitude goes out to these faithful and inspiring people: my mother, Mrs. Zenora Watford, and in loving memory of my father Walter E. Watford, Also to my siblings, Gloria, Barbara, Joyce, David, Larry, and George.

To my motivators, doctors, and teachers in the eastern North Carolina area. Mrs. Phoebe Watson, Dr. William Atkins, Dr. Charles G. Pierce, Mrs. Beverly Riddick, Mrs. Gail Bridges, Mrs. Janet White, Dr. Charles Sawyer, Dr. Brian Magrane, Bishop LeRoy J. Woolard, Freida Clark Cowan, Dr. Peter A. VanHouten, Dr. Steven Steinberg, Dr. Paul Bolin, Dr. Wayne Kendrick, Dr. Graham Byrum, Dr. Earl Capps, and, last but not least, Dr. Stephen Smith.

These are the people who reached out to me when I thought all hope was gone.

Table of Contents

2000

2011

1984

Still Waters

Sitting here by a cozy fire,
thinking of someone I really admire.
You bring me happiness, joy, and glee,
but yet I've never said how much you mean to me.
You haven't told me that you love me,
but I see it in your eyes.
Your look, your touch, your actions
sometimes make me want to cry.
Life isn't a bed of roses, nor as sweet as pie.
That's why we must understand each other or love will die.
Understanding, faith, trust, and love are what we must keep,
It's just like still waters; it runs very deep.

1985

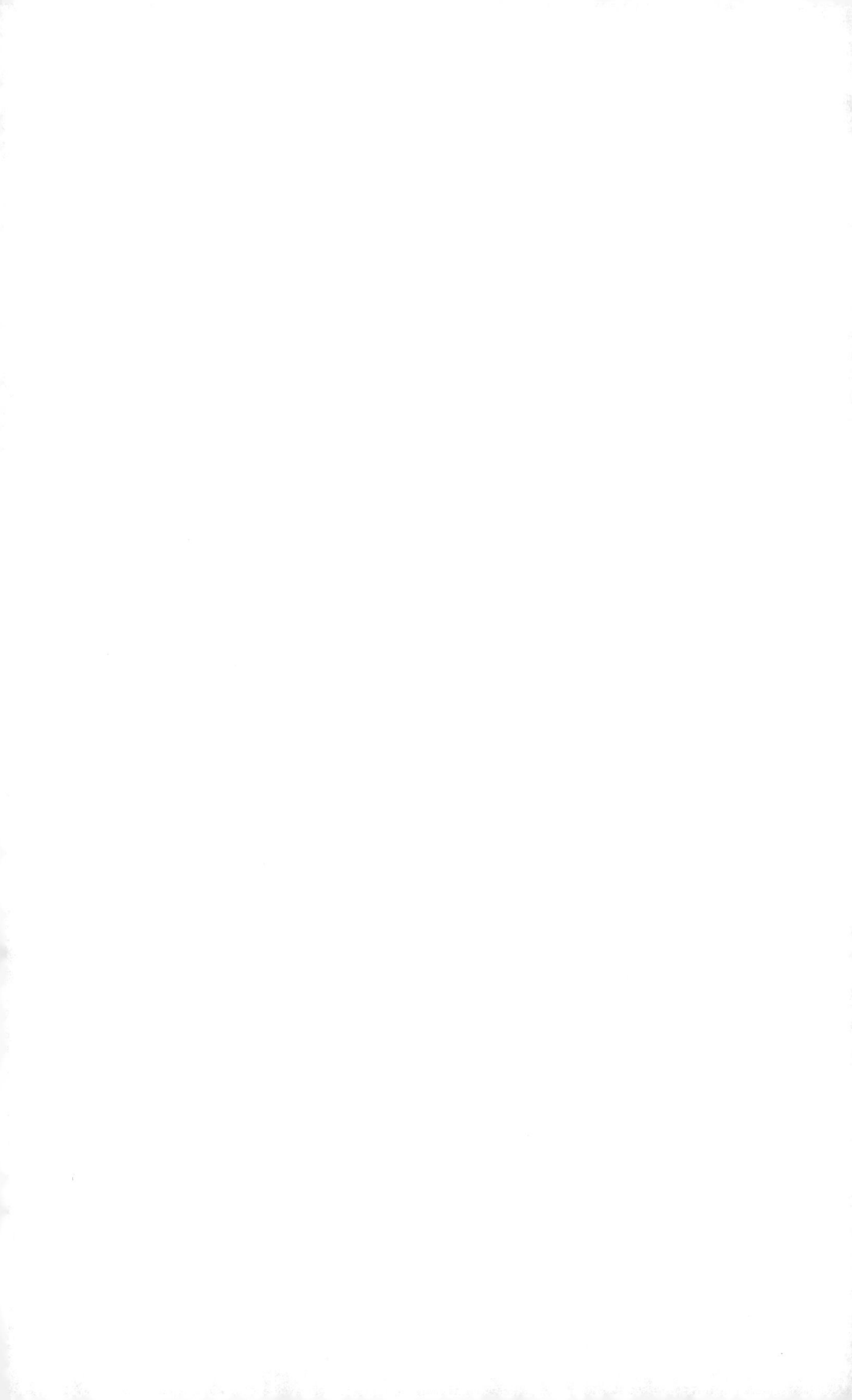

Untitled

If I could influence the world,
with my dignity and charm,
every man, woman, and child alive
would be fully fed and warm.
Their clothes would be nice and clean,
not a lot of expensive things,
but decent ones.
Every man would have a job, secure where
he dwells.
Away with drugs, violence, prejudice, and
other things that are sending us to hell.
Just a vision from heaven; he wants us to
clean up our act.
For neither the day nor the hour is known,
when my savior is to come back!

What Is Love?

What is love?
A question very seldom asked.
Is it just uniting or
fighting to the very last?
Is it talking about the good old times,
or taking life day by day?
Sure enough, one would reply,
love is more than words could possibly say.

1986

Lost Love

Whatever happened to the love we had?
To the hopes, the dreams, and the joy we shared?
Today is the last day we have to share,
and what happens after then I really don't care.
The love we had is no longer there,
but I'll miss him, and I hope he knows I care.
I don't know what happened or where it began,
but of one thing I'm sure: this is the ending.
I knew love couldn't go on forever, but it didn't soften the blow.
I'll never forget that awful day when I told him, "I had to go."

1987

Until the End

When I looked into your eyes, I saw a man.
When we walked out into the rain hand in hand.
The feelings I had for men I thought had gone,
but I realize now that I'm not alone.
For I want to be by your side until the end,
and I want to love you again and again.
For I want to be by your side until the end,
and I want you to know that love never ends.
I will care for you and hold you in my arms.
I will love you till death do us part.
My commitment to you is there,
and our love is one that we'll always share.
I will always be there for you,
even when times are so blue that I don't care.
So remember that, if we happen to go astray,
our love was put right here, to stay ...

What If?

What if I did come back to you? Would it be the same?
What if I did make love to you? Would it change the pain?
If it came to the one you love, would it just be me?
For the love that I desire, it's everlasting!
I gave my all to you: my body, soul, and mind,
and you wasted them extensively.
Now you want me back a second time?
So listen now my brother, I've got myself on track.
There's only one thing left to say:
I'm not coming back.

Smile

A smile is brighter than the most brilliant star,
and sweeps through the most hardened hearts.
Smiles open up the good in the past,
and they also help when you are at your last.
Smiles help relax you at a moment of unease;
they encourage you to stay when you are ready to leave.
Smiles beautify in mysterious ways,
and give life a better look from day to day.
Yes, a smile comes and yes, a smile goes,
but one thing's for sure: it lets people know
you're happy.

A True Friend

A friend is loyal.
A friend is true.
A friend will cheer you up when you are blue.
A friend will stay through thick and thin
and ease the pain that lies within.
They are ones who support our every deed,
although you may be in the wrong.
Though days are short, bright, and beautiful,
they make them seem so long.
What people don't seem to understand is that
a true friend is a friend to the very end.

Do You Love Me?

Take a look around you;
tell me what you see.
Am I the one you love?
Or are you fooling me?
If we ever got together,
as intimate as can be,
would love be forever, or just
one night together?
Tell me that you love me;
show me that you care.
Let love be forever and we'll
spend our lives together.
Times when I feel so all alone,
will you help me to understand
that love isn't wrong?
When problems sometimes come and
seem to get me down,
come to me, take me by the hand,
and show me that love will always stand.
So tell me, do you love me, will you stick by me?
Make me your wife and we'll walk the ways
of love by day and by night.

Going My Own Way

I saw the hurt within your eyes.
How it made me want to break down and cry.
How sorrowful I feel for what has been done.
I feel so bad, for I am the one.
I started to leave; you told me to stay.
It really wasn't my fault that I
was going my own way.
My heart seeped with sorrow,
my eyes filled with tears.
How I wanted to make you mine
and love you through the years.
Guilt is what I feel—why, I don't know.
Maybe I had more concern for you than I let show.
I feel that you are with me all through the day.
For the thought of you is in my mind
as I travel, many miles away.

Going Home

The sun is high, and there are clouds about;
I feel the joy that makes you shout.
My life is full and at a normal pace,
how I'd love to see his loving face.
One day they say he's coming back,
to take his children home.
That will be the day you look for me,
and I'll be gone on home.
They say his home is full of love,
happiness, joy, and glee.
How I want the saints
to join in fellowship with me!

He's the Way to the Promised Land

This man I know,
has the world in his hand.
You know he's the way,
to the promised land.
When you're tired and it seems like
everything is wrong,
just seek my Jesus—he'll make you strong.
He said if you have the faith
of a mustard seed,
you can move any mountain,
any mountain that you please.
Sometimes when trouble
seems to get you down,
just call my savior; he'll be
right there on time.
Oh, he is the way,
yes he is.
He is the way to the promised land.
He is the way to the promised land.

Acceptance

As a part of my life,
as an ending of my worries,
a piece of happiness,
a part of letting go of what isn't mine.
A lover as well as being loved,
taking life one day at a time,
the days as bright as ever.
Making it through the rainy days without tears.
Taking pieces torn apart and proudly
joining them together.
Coping with the hardship of life,
living in a beautiful world of happiness,
dealing with the pressures of mankind.
If I had a chance to make the world,
I would.

Why Did We Have to Love This Way?

My life was full of love.
My heart was set on you
until that day we were set apart.
And I'm so lonely now; it's hard
to keep in control.
Tell me why? Why did you have to go?
Tell me why, why did we have to love this way,
why did we have to break away?
Because I love you …
The nights are cold now;
I really need someone to hold me tight.
Why couldn't we have come together, as
man and wife?
I need you now, I need someone to love
me right, and there's no one. No one can
do that but you.
Tell me why did you have to go away?
Why didn't you come into my arms and stay?
Why did you have to love this way?
Why did we have to break away?
Because I love you …

1993

Wondering

I've been down,
I've been all alone,
wondering if my baby
would come back home.
Did I run you away?
Did I hurt you?
What was it?
Did I make you blue?
I sit here in deep depression,
crying, 'cause I
don't know why.
But I know,
I'm going to keep on,
trying to make everything
all right.
Then maybe he'll come,
he'll come back to me,
and tell me
what I've done wrong.
Oh, I'm wondering in the morning.
Oh, I'm wondering in the middle of the day.
Yes, I'm still wondering if he still loves me,
and I'm wondering if he's coming back to stay.

Knowing

How will I know if I don't take a chance?
How will I know if there will be any romance?
If there are not trials, then how can you fulfill the task?
The wise are weak and the weak are wise.
So, why is it hard to compromise?
You play and get played, you lay and get laid.
It's all a process of knowing …
that life exists after death.
Love exists after hurt.
And after sorrow, happiness always arises.
After knowing, you can live.

Behind the Smile

Even though I smile—
it doesn't mean there's delight.
Just because I laugh a lot—
it doesn't mean happiness is what I share.
I smile to keep away the pain,
and laugh to hold back the cry.
On days when burdens grow inside,
laughing helps me to get by.
Just because I'm smiling—
don't take for granted how I feel.
Smiling is just my way of hiding
pain that is so real!

God Lives

To each of you who knows me,
and to those who even care.
I want you to know, God is real,
and that he's always there.
Just don't look for him across the street,
or even down the block.
My God lives everywhere,
especially within your heart.
He's a man that cures;
you just have to believe.
He's a man that can move mountains,
with the faith of a mustard seed.
Yes my God is real, as real as real can be.
Just yield yourself to him, then sit back, watch, and see.
I've never seen life in such a different way.
Those who live and walk with him
shall rejoice on Judgment Day!

Open Heart

Here I am, Lord, in this sinful world,
and I don't know what to do.
I try so hard to do what's right,
but it just doesn't make it through.
I'm glad to know I have a friend
with an open heart,
and because of his precious love,
he has given me a brand-new start.
Jesus is with me through the day;
he even keeps me through the night.
I must do my very best
to walk with him in the light!

Moving On

I'm tired of the changes.
I'm tired of the games.
You know that life goes on
and that people change.
Why must I go through the agony?
Why must I take the pain?
I'm not the one who hurt you.
I'm not the same.
I tell you, "You hurt my feelings."
And yes, you really do.
I'm getting tired of being hurt,
for it wasn't me who carried you through.
I'm tired of these things I'm feeling.
You're just keeping me hanging on.
Time is winding down,
and when it does,
I'll be gone.

Be Grateful

Every morning that I awake,
how thankful I am.
For God has granted me another day,
to change the way I am.
Why do we take for granted
the many days that he gives?
Without my father's blessings,
another day we would never live.
My father holds the world in the palm of his hand.
If he would put it down, the world would not stand.
The day is coming very soon
when my father will return.
Be yea also ready, so that when it does,
you will never burn.

1994

Cigarettes

Every time you light up one,
think of what could be.
Think of many happy things
that God has planned for thee.
To destroy that demon that lives within me.
To destroy it isn't easy,
and only God can set it free.
So when it comes about, think of God's precious hand
that will deliver you from all evil that the devil has planned.

From Within

I cried to God last night,
and for one good reason. Why,
even though my life is full of joy,
there's still an empty space left inside.
I praise the Lord that fills thy heart,
but there's still an empty part.
What must I do? I don't know,
but for many such as myself,
this feeling grows, and grows, and grows.
Lord, when will this feeling subside?
It hurts within.
Please help me, Lord, to hold out
until the very end.
Lord, now that you have comforted me,
in your own special way,
give me a blessing from up above,
that will fill this space in every way.

In Your Heart

When you are sad and lonely
and feel that no one cares,
read this poem and guess who's there.
You may not see me every day;
I may not even call.
But just remember you're in my heart,
spring, summer, winter, and fall.
Call me not only when you need me,
but also to be a friend.
This kind of love lasts forever
because it lives within.
When I'm down, smile at me and
I'll smile back at you.
When I smile you will know
that you have brought me through.
So when you're sad and lonely
and feeling down and blue,
just read this passage once again,
and I'll be there with you.
In your heart.

1997

Touch Me

When things are not right in my life,
fix it.
Turn my darkness into light.
Lord, fix it.
Fix it Lord, fix it.
Touch me and make me whole.
When sickness comes like it's here to stay,
fix it.
A touch from my master's hand will surely take it away.
Lord, fix it.
Fix it, Lord, fix it.
Touch me and make me whole.

Touch me, Lord.
Father, touch me.
Touch me and make me whole.

1998

Thy Faith Has Made Thee Whole

Through many years of needles
and pricking fingers every day,
something inside kept telling me
the Lord will make a way.
The passing out at night, lying close to death,
how the Lord saw fit to send someone,
to find me and help.
Up the road I traveled and became legally blind.
Another blessing came when the doctors performed
surgery, and once again I could see things shine.
Not forgetting the Lord's words to me, "I will make
thee whole," I just kept the faith and waited for
things to unfold.
Another test I traveled, as I went on the dialysis
machine. Mondays, Wednesdays, and Fridays were
just so hard for me. The many days I cried, "Lord,
please help me."
For a year I fought to keep my sanity and struggled
to keep going on. "Oh Lord, I am weak and my body
is worn."
Then up to heaven I looked, and I began to pray,
"Lord I need some joy, so I can hold on to a life
that I do not enjoy."
Suddenly the phone rang and a lady began
to say, "I'm a nurse calling from Duke and we have two
organs for you."
Soon we were off, the surgery went well, and I'm
doing great now. Thanks to God, I no longer have
diabetes or renal failure!
Thy faith has made me whole.

I've Been Where You Are

Do you see yourself moving from place to place?

Do you find yourself unhappy with your surroundings?

Look at your life; does everything you start become a disaster?

I've been where you are!

Can you remember yourself as a child, and the happiness that lies within?

Without worrying, accepting life as it was.

Your mother making you to go to church and learn the goodness of the Lord.

I've been where you are!

Suddenly you were old enough to make decisions of your own.

You began to hang out all night, dancing in the clubs, drinking, smoking, committing adultery or fornication, and thinking you're having a good time.

Hey! I've been where you are!

Then you woke up one day, after years have passed, to discover life has served you nothing.

You're not happy, you're broke, and you have accomplished nothing.

I've been where you are!

Then you remembered your life as a child, and you look at yourself now.

There's only one thing missing in your life, and that's our Lord and savior,

Jesus Christ.

I've been where you are!

But just as I began to pray, I heard a knock at my soul.

A voice began to say to me, "Come as you are Christ is the way.

No more waiting, no more running. Now is the time."

I lifted my hands and asked my savior to come in.

I've been where you are!

Some people take for granted God's mercy and grace,

but I tell you now that Christ is the way.

Not every day will be like roses, for trials come and go.

These trials are for teaching us; that's how we grow.

Through it all, one must say that there's light to see where you've

been, and light to help you continue to the very end.

I've been where you are!

Now that God has granted you life, let's not

go back to those things that have kept us bound.

Just keep the faith, and magnify the Lord, for he's the one who

unbound you, and much, much, more …

Stay encouraged. Come what may, keep the faith, and endure to the

end,

and we'll shout together on Judgment Day.

I've been where you are!

Who Am I?

For many years I wondered,
what would I ever be?
Why do I do the things I do
and still think of the almighty king?
Is there a reason that I'm here?
Can someone help me to see?
What am I to do?
Is there still a special place for me?
As the years went by, I began to understand.
Being a child of God, that's his number-one plan.
I sinned because that's what the natural
man will do. Until the day I accepted Christ,
and he washed me through and through.
That's why I think of Christ,
because he actually lives within.
My purpose is to spread the news of Jesus,
who died for our sins.
Only God can tell you and make you
what and whom you are supposed to be.
So what am I to do?
God's will;
and by doing that, he'll give you the desires
of your heart and set your burdens free.
There is a place for you and me,
and that's in heaven above.
By doing God's will from day to day
and showing others his everlasting love,
I'm a child of the king.

Shower Me

Fill me with happiness,
soothe me with cheer.
Bless me, Lord, to see another year.
Fill my heart with joy;
fill my life with peace.
Teach me, Lord, to be obedient so I can
have life and live it more abundantly.
Fill me with thy holy spirit;
walk with me through the day.
Shower me with your unconditional love,
that I may share it
in each and every way.
Fill me with forgiveness.
Teach me how to care.
Shower me with blessings,
so that I can bless someone else.
To sum it all up, Lord,
this is what I ask of you.
Shower me with all those things
that will make me perfect unto you.

Reaching Out

There's something I see
from far away.
It makes me happy
from day to day.
To reach out and touch it
would please me, dear.
Just a few moments
to hold it near.
How do I make it mine
all the time,
instead of at a blink of an eye?
What am I doing wrong?
Did I not capture it within?
Another moment I held it tight,
then suddenly it was gone.
So what do I do now?
Watch from afar,
because what may seem right
just may be wrong.

1999

My Heart

Many times you've wondered
how someone really feels.
Are you just pretending?
Or is it more than just a thrill?
What are you looking for,
or what is it that you see?
Can I trust you with my feelings,
or should I just let things be?
Sometimes I wonder if you really know.
The pain from the past
makes it harder to let go.
It's not that I'm not who I say I am;
I just want to be sure that you're for real
and not just saying things that I adore.
Being hurt again is one thing
I don't want, that's true.
Not only do I not want to be hurt,
but I don't want to hurt you.
Yes, I see your needs,
and I understand them too,
but to pour my feelings out to you—
I'm sorry—that's something I can't do.
So, just in case you didn't see it,
at that moment you turned away,
I took the love I held within me,
 and put it on display.

Will You Care For Me?

Will you care for me?
If I seem to be strange, if I don't enjoy
clubbing, smoking, drinking—those kinds
of things—
will you care for me?
Especially when I work all the time,
trying to build a better life for you
and me.
Will you accept me for who I am,
and not what you want me to be?
Although I may be a herdsman,
will you be happy with me, just being me?
For if I was a shepherd and suddenly lost
my sheep, would you help me to find them,
or just sit and watch me weep?
Now truly, if you cared for me,
you'd stand by me through thick and thin,
not walking away when things look dim.
So just being who I am,
with a glimmer of hope,
will you face life's challenges with me,
or leave me hanging without a rope?

Where Do I Stand?

On Judgment Day, when the trumpet sounds,
where will I be?
Will I be caught up in the rapture,
or awaiting hell's door,
bound and enslaved?
Will I acknowledge my sins
before that final day,
and ask the Lord for forgiveness
so I can rejoice and praise his name,
in each and every way?
When my name is called,
is this what the Lord will say to me?
"Depart from me, I know you not,
you worker of iniquity,
you did not adhere to thy word."
Or will he say instead,
"Well done, my good and faithful servant.
Enter into the gates, for you
have kept all my commandments."
So where do I stand in judgment?
Have I done all that I know to do?
For if I haven't done these things,
Lord, help me to get these commandments
right with you!

No Turning Around

Just when I thought it was over,
here comes 'ole Satan again.
Poking, probing, and trying to steal my joy
and to bring back the old man.
Although I am human, and yes sometimes I
fall down, here's a little reminder
Satan, that God is still in charge and
I'm not turning back around.
Sometimes these things happen just to
test your faith.
You've gone through many trials, and have
suffered many days, but one thing you
must know Satan—God has always made a way.
God did not come when I wanted him to, but
when he came he was right on time.
That's why my focus has stayed on pleasing God,
and Satan, there's no turning back around.

Let's Get High Together

I woke up this morning
thinking of how to do wrong,
and a voice began to say to me,
"Why do yourself harm?"
Of course I didn't listen,
and began to take a puff,
when suddenly I began coughing up
some smelly brown stuff.
"Go to the doctor," the little voice said,
and once again I overlooked this warning.
As the day progressed, I started to drink,
and once again, I heard this voice say,
"Don't let your life sink."
This could never happen to me, I thought.
Just then the voice said,
"Look at your friends; that's what they thought
before they took their fall. They thought this
life was good and never did they think of me.
Satan showed them hell and no way out, you see.
Before you take that next drink for the day, remember
that I am the Lord thy God, I am the way.
I bring life that never has to end.
I'm also the peace and joy you want within.
So, before you take that last and final drink,
give your heart to me. I'll give you peace and
joy, and most of all, life and it more abundantly."

Spiritual Awareness

When you hear a little voice saying,
"Don't go," or "That's wrong,"
just remember that's the Lord keeping you from harm.
When you feel guilty, that's the Lord as well.
He convicts us in our hearts to get it right,
then you won't go to hell.
That constant little voice, that's saying those
things to you, It's just a reminder from God,
that he's always there with you.
Never neglect to hear him, just come when he calls.
This voice you hear from heaven above will
never let you fall.
In case you don't know who's talking,
it's the Almighty King.
He'll give you joy so you can laugh, shout, and sing.

Do You Know Me?

Do you really know me?
Just who am I?
I awake you every morning,
so why do you cry?
When times are rough and you
don't want to go on,
who gives you the insight
to keep moving on?
So, do you really know me?
For all the things I've done for you.
For if you really knew me, you
would trust in me instead of you.
Who brought you out of Egypt?
Who healed the sick and raised the dead?
For this entire world is mine and
I hold it in my hands.
You pray to me regularly from day to day,
but do you really know who I am?
I am the Christ, I am the way.
So now get to know me,
and yield yourself totally, you see.
I will then give you life,
and set your burdens free.

Life

Don't take for granted what you have;
it's not promised every day.
The same way the Lord gives,
surely, he can take it away.
Those things we treasure,
our homes and our cars,
are they really more precious than life?
Life comes once in the bodily man,
so take care of it the best you can.
Don't let the devil fool you,
open your eyes and see.
Christ is the one who loves you.
He'll supply your every need.
So, don't let the devil fool you;
put down those drugs and pray.
So when you die the second time,
you can look back and say,
"I made it."

What it's All About

It's not about all of my possessions, and
it's not about what I may or may not gain.
Surely it's not about all of your fortune,
nor is it about your fame.
It's not about how pretty you can be, nor
is it about your shape, you see?
Indeed, it's not about your home or your car.
Just in case you didn't know, it's about
the love of Christ within your heart.
Yes, it's all about Jesus and carrying his
spoken word—these things are commanded of us
to give to all what needs to be heard.
How they crucified him on the cross,
by the driving of nails into his hands.
Jesus did this for us, that we may live again.
How they speared him in his side
and left him there to die.
But on the third day, he rose again, with
all powers in his hand.
Yes, Jesus did this all for us!
Now confess your sins,
believe that Jesus died and rose again.
Ask him to come into your heart;
then you'll receive a brand new start,
in the love of Jesus Christ.

Playing Games

Just because I say to you,
this is what I do,
Please take note, check me out,
and see if this is true.
Although I may come by regularly
or call you every day,
this could be only a plot,
to get things going my way.
I may take you to the finest of restaurants
and have you stay a couple of nights.
These things I must do,
to make sure my plan goes just right.
Watch me closely, listen to my every word.
Just remember, I'm going to slip
and say something that will make you
really disturbed.
Pay attention to my movements; call me unexpectedly.
Take note of all my actions, then
sit back, watch, and see.
Somewhere down the line, I will eventually
make a mistake.
Because trying to play two women in safety
can never take place.
Carefully watch my actions and once again,
watch my moods. Sooner or later I'll goof up
and will have to tell the truth.
Now that I am busted
and got caught in my own mischief,
never again will I be trusted.

So, all I know to do is weep.
I've lost someone that was so dear to me,
just because I was playing games,
instead of being truthful about myself
and the situation that remains.
I'm sorry, is what I wish to say, but will
it soften the blow? She slowly walks
away saying, "Honey I've got to go.
No more heartache, no more pain, I'm leaving
you now, so you do the best you can."

Reflections

When I look back over my life and see
all those things I've done,
"Oh! What a disgusting sight," I must say,
although I knew that they were wrong.
Just to looking back makes me so thankful
now, for God has yet delivered me.
No more cursing; it doesn't look hot.
Cursing gives you an ugly character,
especially when you're not.
No more smoking; it gives you cancer of the
lungs. The alcohol kills your brain cells,
and does the liver much harm.
No more fornication; this kills your spiritual
soul. You then take on other peoples' habits;
sometimes it makes you lose control.
How great to understand the sick in so many
different ways—how they feel mistreated, and
some of the horrible things nurses can say.
Just to know how Job felt, when he could
have cursed the day he was born. People say
they understand, but until you've been
there yourself like Job and I, believe me,
you're wrong.
All these things I've gone through have helped
me grow through the years. Those things make
you mature and help you to give others in
life some strength, hope, and cheer.
Once again, I thank the Lord in my heart, soul,
and mind. He gave me the strength, peace, and

joy that I tried so hard to find.
I thank my mother for teaching me
the right way to go, although I
strayed for many years, I kept Jesus
in my soul.
I also thank my second mom, she's so dear
to me too. She encourages me also to
do what's right and to keep pressing my way
through.
To all of those I've encountered, through
this journey from beginning to end, your
prayer, blessings, and contributions will
always be kept within.
For all the love you've shown me, I see it
every day, and once again I thank you, and
will keep you in prayer.
I'll love you always.

Keep Pressing On

Now that my journey's over,
don't think of me as passed away.
I do live again in Yahweh,
and will arise on Judgment Day.
This world was only temporary,
that I may save mine and help
others to save their souls.
My work was then completed;
I'd reached a number untold.
I'm resting in my father's bosom—
this is where I belong.
To you I say, keep the faith and
keep pressing on.

What a Joy

What a joy it is to find someone
Who loves the Lord too.
Just to sit back, laugh, sing
and to praise him through and
through.
What a joy it is to know that
someone else really cares, how
you acknowledge the Lord in every
thing and everywhere.
What a joy it is to know that
there's prepared a special place,
for God's children after they
have fought a good fight and
run a good race.
What a joy it is to know that on
that final day, that my God will arise
and every knee shall bow, with the
confession that Christ is Lord.
What a joy it is to know that the
Lord has given us time to get cleansed
of our sins.
Now the time is getting
near for my God to come again.
What a joy to know that right at
this time, you can confess all your
sins and be made new again.
Now that these joys are known within,
stop waiting and come back to an
everlasting friend!

I Just Wanted You to Know

Although I may be gone
to a land far away,
just remember my love for you
is always here to stay.
Remember the times I held you tight
and kept you close, my dear.
That closeness still lives within us,
so pick up your head and look at those things
we've accomplished through the years.
Can't you feel the wind blowing across your
face? Remember honey, that's me! Pushing your
hair behind your ears, holding you with a
strong embrace.
Sometimes when you smell the fragrance of my
cologne, that's just to remind you that you're
not alone.
You thought you heard some footsteps, well,
that was me, too. I just had to come by and
check up on you.
I would like to stay for tea with you, but I
know it's not so. So, I'll observe you from across
the table, before to work you go.
All these things I remind you are just to let
you know that everything you do and everywhere
you go—my presence is always with you.
I just wanted you to know.

Walking Away

When I walked away,
you were put into my past.
Not a tear did I shed,
not a grumble, not a word.
To leave with a smile
lets you know I had cheer.
For all my questions were answered
with complicity instead of fear.
In my heart, the truth was already known;
it was just a point of making every
deception known.
So after all of this,
what's left to be said?
Maybe you should have told me, instead.
You show up unannounced;
I'm sure to speak soft, pleasant words.
I'm mighty afraid of what I didn't say
now will be heard.
So now to step back in my life,
playing those games of yesteryear.
You need to get a life and learn how
to maintain it, my sweet dear.
Oh! Yes you tried to play me
and I convinced you to go on,
but little did you know that you were trying
to con a con.
It never would have worked out,
and I guess by now you see.
Just when you thought I'd left,

I quickly turned back around,
only to catch you with your guard down.
I tried so hard to warn you,
but you kept looking the other way.
Just when you realized what I'd said,
Oops ... too late, I had turned and walked away.

Yeshuwa

The founder of Christianity,
the Alpha, the first,
and the Omega, the last.
I am the beginning,
and I am the ending.
Whosoever believeth in me
should not perish, but have everlasting life.
I am everlasting strength.
I shall be unto you an everlasting light,
and Yah thy glory.
For those who know not Yeshuwa
and obey not the gospel of Yah
shall be punished, with everlasting destruction,
from the presence of Yah and from the glory
of his power.
But whosoever shall deny me before men,
him I will also deny before my father (Yahweh).
Which is in heaven?
Hallelujah, praise Yah.

Who Is He?

Who is this man? Who made man in
his own image, whose designating
knowledge is beyond the limits of
all life?
Who is he, that's pure in spirit and
unlimited in time and space?
That's eternal, all-knowing, and all-powerful?
Who is he?
He is imminent, who pervades everything,
and is infinitely exalted above the
universe.
Among all of this, he's personal,
rational, self-conscious, self-
determining, and an intelligent moral
being.
He has compassion in times of
sickness, grace in the presence of
guilt, and he is also sovereign.
His life is eternally within himself
and consists of a fellowship
of three equal and distinct persons.
Yah the father, Yah the son, and
Yah the Holy Spirit holy spirit.
Who is he?
I am that I am.
Yahweh.

Go Away

Why do you call me?
Are you trying to stay near?
Why come by to see me
when your life is far from clean?
Why try to make me promises that we both
know you can't keep?
So why abuse yourself,
knowing that you can't convince me?
Why keep fooling yourself, when you tell me
you're back on the right track?
Of course, you know that without the Lord,
you're just telling a bunch of lies.
So listen to me closely;
understand exactly what I'm going to say.
The feelings I had from first we met
have now gone away.

So You Say

So you say you know God,
but I don't think you do.
For if you really knew him,
you would want to hear what the
Bible says to do.
Can you truly call yourself a saint
when you don't want to hear what's right?
Surely a true servant knows
we walk by faith and not by sight.
You let the devil fool you
when he showed you the couple that's happy and glad,
but when you spent the night that happiness turned sad.
It wasn't what you expected.
You saw something that wasn't there.
That's 'ole Satan's deception.
That's why we should always
pray, rejoice, and be glad.
Yes, we pray for husbands and wives too,
but are we qualified for the responsibilities
that each one has to do.
You stay home with your mother,
and she's the one who cleans your room.
Trust me, you don't need a husband;
your mother does.
The meals that you cook will help a lot.
Just remember—a wife consists of a whole lot more,
whether you know it or not.
Do you have a budget plan to help him save,
or are you looking through his wallet, saying,

"Oh boy! I can go shopping today"?
The Lord knows his perfect design,
and if you're not ready,
then it's just not your time.
So stop looking for that perfect one,
for he's not for you to find.
Seek yea first the kingdom of God,
and all his righteousness, then delight
thyself also in the Lord; and he shall give
thee the desires of your heart.

Keep Holding On

When times get rough
and things are going wrong,
help me, Lord, to keep the faith,
and to keep pressing on.

Although your happiness may seem
far away, just pick up your head
and begin to pray.

The Lord knows all of our problems,
and in everything he cares. Just say
"Thank you Lord for all you've done,"
and know he's always there.

For everything that happens, Lord,
there's a reason, I know. Just help
me to see your purpose, so I can
help someone else to grow.

God, I know you don't come right
when I want you to, but you're
always on time. Just give me
the patience, hope, and strength,
to keep holding on to words divine.

No Turning Around

When I was young, I stayed sick a lot,
and many times wanted to die. Not once did
my savior allow it, so I just suffered and cried.

During my sickness, I continued to pray, and I
conquered the battles that kept coming my way.

As a teen, the many years I struggled through
school and kept trying to do my best—
for all those years I'd shed many tears, but to accomplish
my goals was my number-one test.

After graduating high school, I slowly drifted
away from my first love, Yah, and singing in the church where
I found fellowship and prayer.

Many years later, while hanging in the streets condemnation,
something shook me, and I began to awaken from a dead sleep.

My life wasn't happy anymore; it was the same old thing.
The promises, lies, deceptions, and beating of others at their
own game.

How I don't want this life anymore, there must be a better
way. Just when I began to rimiest, and I thought of the good
old days.

For many years I sang of the precious Yah, to others
they call Lord, my life was full of happiness, and never
was I bored.

I had lost fellowship with my savior, the one who died
for my sins. Oh, Yah, take me back that I may live again.

Just as I heard Yah knocking, slowly I opened the door.
Just at that instant, my change came aboard.

My burdens were then lifted; I could see a new light ahead.
How thankful to have a forgiving savior, who will forgive
the ones who are living but dead.

Not every day is sunny, but there's always that glimpse of
light. Know that Yah is always there to help you do what's right.

Although for many years I ran the wrong way, but I tell
you now from where I stand, "no turning back," I must say.

Best Friends

Just to see the smiles you bring when you come in,
omitting all sorrow and pain that had lied so long within.
How you shower your love and concern for others, each and
every day.
Never giving up, just keeping the faith, and going your own way.
Determined to keep peace, and striving to do what's right.
Although our days get cloudy sometimes, you keep standing
strong, walking that straight and narrow way that sometimes
seems so long.
Verification of the Lord's presence you give, and you top it
off with a smile. This suddenly brings back the tender light
the clouds tried so hard to hide.
It's good to know that there is a friend with a sincere heart.
Sharing, serving, and helping. What a man, who does a lot.

The Lord's Mighty Wind

The Lord's mighty wind, how it blows so strong.
Job says it's sometimes for correction, or
   even his land alone.
Only God knows, he's never wrong.
How we shut up everything from his wind
   and rain.
Truly if my father wanted,
   he'd undo it just the same.
For all his glorious wonders,
   we don't thank him enough.
Instead we want his mighty works to go away
   and forget his purposes for us.
Never do we look beyond his wonders,
   shown from day to day.
We ignore it once again,
   and continue going the same old way.
He's trying to capture our attention,
   and this is what he's saying to me:
"Come back home my children,
   praise me, on bended knees."
How merciful my father is, to let us remain
   through all his strong wind and rain.
He could have allowed destruction, for all of you to see,
   but once again he blessed you as well as me.
So be thankful for my father's work,
   whether to you, it may be good or bad.
For God has a purpose for everything,
   just thank him and be glad.

Open Your Eyes

Have you ever known a time when you were really,
really sad, but deep down within, you were happy and glad?
Although I now live without car or home, I thank you,
Yahweh, just the same, for keeping me alive, fully
fed, and warm.
The many things I've worked for, by the sweat of my
brow. It was only temporary, not only for then, but
even for now.
This is only a lesson for me to see, that those
treasures will not set my soul free.
When I got caught up in my treasures, I became blind
and couldn't see that those special things I wanted
changed my attitude inside.
I couldn't see myself, as my friends slowly drifted
away. It wasn't because of what I had, but it was my
attitude that I began to carry day by day.
I've yet learned a great lesson from this storm and
its rain, and that's to always stay the same regardless
of what you may or may not gain.

I Don't Have to Cry

I don't have to cry no more, for God has washed my sins away.
I don't have to cry no more because he showed me a brighter day.
I don't have to cry no more, for he gave me the victory.

When troubles seeps my mind, all I'm to do is pray and ask
the Lord to help me to make it through another day.
I don't have to cry, for the Lord stands by me.
I don't have to cry, for he gives me the victory.

Just as I was walking, a voice said unto me, "Come, join my
family, and I'll show you that better way." You don't have to
cry, for he'll wash your sins away. You don't have to cry.

Chorus 1
I don't have to cry no more,
for he washed my sins away.
I don't have to cry because he showed me a brighter day.
I don't to cry, for he gave me the victory.
I don't have to cry.

Be Real

You call yourself fly, and
you think you look good.
Surely if you'd put the same expense
into your personality, you'd look a
whole lot better than good.
You say you envy others,
but they really don't care.
For to listen, to respect, and to bless
others, is all they care.
They were taught to depend on Yahweh,
for he owns everything.
When their day of old age comes, he'll
bless them just the same.
Man can't give you happiness, nor can he
give you life.
Just a little reminder to you,
having much and having all, without Yahweh,
you're still not content.
So, stop envying others, and start trying to
be a blessing instead.
Despising what others have is getting you
nowhere, you see.
Pull yourself from that crowd at the bottom
of the hill.
Ask Yah for guidance, to move you up slowly
in his will. So, just because you envy others,
don't make them despise you, too. For they'll
add some extra prayer, when on bended knees,
for you.
For whatever you want to be, take this in stride.
Put Christ first and he'll direct your life.

He'll Give to You

He'll give you peace in the valley
      among all men.
He'll give you peace in the valley
      that lives within.
Just acknowledge my savior
      and ask him to come in.
Broken hearts are his specialty
      and he wants to mend.

He'll give you peace in the valley
      among all men.
He'll give you peace in the valley
      that lives within.
He'll supply your every need;
      all you have to do is believe.
So give your heart to Jesus;
      he'll supply you with peace.

Give your heart to Jesus,
      for he loves you so.
Give your heart to Jesus
      and never let him go.
He'll supply your every need;
      all you have to do is believe.
So give your heart to Jesus;
      he'll supply you with peace.

No Turning Back

If you don't want to know the truth,
don't call me.
If you don't want to hear what's right,
don't talk to me.
If you don't want to hear the word,
stay away from me.
For I'm living my life for the Lord.

I've stumbled many times along the way.
I had obstacles I could not break from day to day.
But the Lord washed me clean that I might praise his name.
And no turning back, I want to say.

Many trials and tribulations help me find my way.
My eyes were opened to the games Satan tried to play.
But the Lord brought me out that I may show someone the way.
And no turning back, I want to say.

Accept The Truth

Why do you accept false doctrine?
Is it because you want to do what you
want to do?
Why do you come to linger at my house?
Is it because you want to find fault in
me too?
How is it that you can talk about faith
and can't explain Romans 5:2?
So why do you come to talk to me?
Just to convince me that your way is true?
How you try to convince me of your Lord's words,
but when I pull out my Bible, your mouth opens
and not a sound is heard.
"Is this right?" you ask. "Is this God
speaking, and is it so?"
I'm mighty afraid it is. So why hasn't your
pastor told you so? I'm quite sure he knows.
I've read it from the Holy Bible and there's
nothing left to be said.
God holds the world in his hand. If you don't
abide, then you cannot stand.
For we will be judged by the book, not by what
you heard me say. That's why we must show ourselves
approved, so that we might stand on
Judgment Day.
You told me that you were coming back with scripture,
and this is what I say to you. If you're not reading
from the Holy Bible, then I'm not wasting time with you.
So ask your pastor these questions, and if he can't
answer you so, then ask the Lord to direct you to the
church where you need to go.

Silly Women

"Hey pretty lady, you're so fine.
I would like you to be mine and only mine."
This is what I tell them, those young and silly girls.
All I want is my fire cooled and my toes twirled.
Those tender honeybees and yes, so fine.
    All I want is what they have inside.
I don't care about how they feel or how they think.
All I need is their love, every time I wink.
Never would I marry them or take them out for show.
They're just my little playthings, and when I'm done,
    out the door I go.
Of course I tell them I love them, that's to keep them
    hanging on.
Until I find my next pretty young thing, then I'll
    just leave this one alone.
I don't care about these honeybees; I use them to satisfy
    my needs.
But the ones that keep us truly happy are those
    that are not in the street.
I say this to you little honeybees: we men mean you no good.
Go back home to the ones who really love you and make
    yourself a life for good.

Crying Out

One day while burdened, Satan encouraging me to do
wrong. I decided to take a drive for an hour or two.

My destination ended; I was standing at my sister's door.
Although I was there, my soul was still low. "Come on in,"
she said. "You're just in time. I'm on my way to church.
Don't you want to drive me and a friend of mine?"

"No," I replied. "I don't have a dress," but deep down inside
I was thinking, I'm not going to stop doing my mess.

Out of the closet came a dress, and then I responded, "I don't
have any shoes." Oh boy, what did I say that for?
She had a pair of those, too.

My excuse was no more, I had an outfit that I had never
worn before.

I've always respected my sisters, whether I listened or not
to what they had to say, but all I could think in mind was, why in
the world am I going to church with them today?

It's already hot I thought, now I have to listen to them
shout and sing. I know I've lost my mind because I could
be doing a whole lot of other things.

I parked across the street and we walked slowly to this small
church. It sounded as if service was great, but I thought I was
making a mistake.

As I walked in and took a seat, a peace came over me and Satan then let go of me.

When the pastor called, I was drawn near to lift my hands with acceptance, and to say thank you Lord, for being so dear.

That other side of me stayed in the chair with my head hung down, but I didn't care, for my burdens were gone and so was my frown. Hey, I was a different being when I left that town.

It was no mistake. For that hour or so drive, only the Lord knew how I really felt inside. Sometimes we don't understand the when or the where, but God knows all and, where he wants you to go, somehow you'll get there.

It doesn't matter how you're thinking, it doesn't matter what you've done, but what really matters is that God forgives, saves lost souls, and now, Satan, you're back on the run.

So the next time that you're out for an hour or two drive, check yourself and see if you're running from what's really inside.

A Question of Life

1   Has John the Baptist come to you saying, repent yea, for heaven is at hand?

2   Did you reject the same stone that the builders rejected?

3   Are you doing violence and accusing man falsely?

4   Are you content with life?

5   Have you filled your vessels with oil?

6   Have you kept Yahweh's way and have not departed from him?

7   Do you walk upright, work righteousness, and speak the truth?

8   Are you backbiting with your tongue?

9   Have you taken reproach against thy neighbor?

10 Do you swear when you become angry?

11 Have you taken reward against the innocent and put this money to usury?

If you can answer yes to questions one, four, five, six, and seven only, you are truly preparing for the return of Christ.

Untitled

It's lonesome when you don't come around.
I'm enjoying your company when you come in town.
Not a week has passed where you haven't called.
It makes me wonder whether you have feelings at all.
You confide in me your thoughts of things you wish to do.
Are these sincere thoughts for me and you?
I've truly begun to care, for I've always liked you so.
But what I'm feeling now, I don't seem to know.
Is there something inside that's been hidden for some time?
Maybe I'm just fooling myself, since there's no other in my life.
Years ago, we both walked away. Are we once again trying to
        right what was left from yesterday?
I think I'll just be silent and let nature take its course.
Love is something you mustn't enforce.

2000

Love

Love began with the betrayal of a kiss.
Led to Caiaphas, to Pilate, then into judgment
      by the Hebrews.
Love accepted the scarlet robe, the scourge, the
plaited crown that was placed on his head,
      and the reed in his right hand.
They then smote him saying, "Hail King of the Jews."
And after they spit on him, smote him, took off his
      robe, and smote him on the head.
Away they took him to be crucified.
Love gave no answer, and once again Jesus was seated in
      the judgment seat in Golgotha.
Love bared his cross and went to Golgotha
Here a title was put o the cross written in Hebrew,
      Greek, and Latin,
"Jesus of Nazareth, the King of the Jews."
After Jesus asked for water and they gave him vinegar,
      he said, "It is finished," and he bowed his head
      and gave up the ghost.
One of the soldiers then, with his spear, pierced him
in his side and forthwith came there out blood
      and water.
Love carried the cross to Golgotha,
where he bled and died.
Each step taken was for you and me,
that we may live again, in Christ Jesus.

Untitled

Why do you call when you know I'm not home?
Should I leave you a schedule, so you'll
know when I'm alone?
I tell you to jot down a few lines when you're
not occupied.
So far you haven't done so, and I realize I'm
just wasting my time.
I understand the surprise visit tactic, but there's
one thing that I must say.
Unless you're very, very, early or very, very, late,
without notification there will be much delay.
I do not have any children, and no man to call
my own.
So I do what I do best, stay away from home.
I have polished my holy armor, then out to seek a
a lost soul, through songs and poetry given from
the Lord.
Just to see the encouragement, joy, and most of
all, uplifted hearts—these things inspire me to
continue my spiritual walk.
This is just a small portion of the love I wish to
give, but most of all to encourage the sick, to fight to live.

He's Coming Back

He's coming back again, yea.
He's coming back again, yea.
He's on his way back now to defend
this world, of all those things that are
sending us to hell.

He's coming back again.
He's coming back again.
He's going to heal the sick.
He's going to raise the dead.
Every knee shall bow and every tongue
shall confess.

He's coming back again.
He's coming back again.

No more pain or sorrow,
no more hate or deceit,
no more aching hearts.
Away with all inequities.

He's coming back again, yea.
He's coming back again.
He's on his way back now to defend
this world, of all those things that are
sending us to hell.
He's coming back again, yea.
He's coming back again.

Why Do I Praise Him?

Do I praise him for his kindness
        or do I praise him for his love?
Is it just to get those special blessings
        that he has promised me from up above?
Do I praise him for his mercy,
        and do I praise him for his grace?
Because I know already that next week
        I'm going to say something that
        will be out of place.
Did someone say this is what you're supposed
        to do? And I did to satisfy man.
But deep within my heart I didn't understand the
        who, what, why, or when.
Did I clap my hands and say *thank you Lord*,
        so you would think that I truly loved him so?
Or did I praise him because I had nowhere else to go?
Did I praise him because I was frightened?
Or did I praise him because my heart
        was full of joy?
Did I have to be brought down so low
        before I could pick up my head and say,
"Save me Lord, take my hand, grant me another
        chance to live again. I'll praise your name" ?
So, am I praising him for my future mansion
        in the sky?
Truly, one would think you'd praise him
        for just being the almighty on high.

Don't Go Away

Just to hear your voice
when you were asked to come in.
That warm and gentle hug you gave
as you walked cautiously in.
How grateful to see you,
your presence has made my day.
That same feeling from first we met,
was put back on display.
The sweat rolled down my face
from that tender kiss and warm embrace—
it's happening all over again,
those same feelings that I hid within.
How I want you to stay;
don't go away.
I'll miss you, dear, for not being near.
Please don't go,
for I do love you so.
I just wanted you to know.

What's Your Excuse for Not Serving God?

I wasn't ready!

(John 7:6) Then Jesus said unto them, my time
is not yet come! But your time is always ready.

My family forsaken me!

(Psalms 27:10) When my father and mother forsake
me, the Lord will take me up.

My job had me stressed out!

(Matthew 11:28) Come unto me, all ye that are
labor and are heavy laden, and I will give you
rest.

It's hard to do the right thing!

(Matthew 11:30) For my yoke is easy, and my burden
is light.

Honestly, I was confused.

(1 Cor 14:33) For God is not the author of confusion,
but of peace as in all churches of the
saints.

I'm not ready to give up worldly pleasures!

(Titus 2:12) Teaching us that, denying ungodliness
and worldly lust, we should live soberly, righteously
and Godly, in this present world.

I was trying to get what Bob has!

(1 Cor 12:31) But covet earnestly the best gifts:
and yet show I unto you a more excellent way.

So, what's your excuse?

(Romans 1:20) For the invisible things of him
from the creation of the world are clearly seen,
being understood by the things that are made, even
his eternal power and godhead; so that they are
without excuse.

2011

I Just Want to Be Loved

I just want to be loved by someone with a gentle, loving hand.
Someone with wisdom and a future in his plans.
I just want to be loved by someone who recognizes responsibilities.
In case of sickness, I can learn to depend on
him, and he can depend on me.
I just want to be loved by someone with sincere words,
whose thoughts and ambitions just can't wait to be heard.
To love me for just who I am with no doubt and concern.
Can you be the one to love me, a real, godly man?

www.ingramcontent.com/pod-product-compliance
Lightning Source LLC
Chambersburg PA
CBHW022024170526
45157CB00003B/1347